The Jewish Diabetes Cookbook

Beulah-Rose Gross

SALLY MILNER PUBLISHING

MILNER HEALTH SERIES

For Rachi
Whose love sustains me

First published in 2001 by
Sally Milner Publishing Pty Ltd
PO Box 2104
Bowral NSW 2576
AUSTRALIA

© Beulah-Rose Gross 2001

Design by Anna Warren, Warren Ventures Pty Ltd, Sydney
Illustrations by Anna Warren, Warren Ventures Pty Ltd, Sydney

Edited by Lyneve Rappell
Photography by Sergio Santos

Printed in Australia

National Library of Australia Cataloguing-in-Publication data:
Gross, Beulah-Rose, 1937–.
    The Jewish diabetes cookbook.

    Includes index.
    ISBN 1 86351 270 5.

    1. Diabetes - Diet therapy - Recipes.
    2. Diabetes - Nutritional aspects. 3. Cookery, Jewish. I. Title.
    (Series : Milner health series).

    641.56314

**Special thanks to Carina Cox of Peppercorn in Berrima, NSW,
for allowing us to photograph items for the cover**

Disclaimer
The information in this instruction book is presented in good faith. However, no
warranty is given, nor results guaranteed, nor is freedom from any patent to be
inferred. Since we have no control over the use of information contained in this book,
the publisher and the author disclaim liability for untoward results.

Foreword

Healthy Eating for People with Diabetes

Food must not only taste good, for people with diabetes it must also be good for blood glucose control. This collection of recipes will help you prepare a menu that is, on balance, low in fat (particularly saturated fat), which is important with diabetes.

Regarding carbohydrate in diabetic diets, we now have better knowledge about those carbohydrates that are preferable. Some carbohydrate foods are digested quickly, leading to rapid rises in blood glucose, while others are moderate in effect. Others are slowly digested. Foods can now be rated in their affect on blood glucose, and this rating is known as The Glycaemic Index (GI). See an Accredited Practising Dietitian (APD) to catch up on the latest research—how you eat can make a difference.

Losing weight

Energy reduction is important to many overweight people, including those with diabetes. Sugars, such as cane sugar, honey and fruit juice concentrates, in a recipe are part of the total carbohydrate and kilojoule (calorie) content, and reducing the amount of these will lead to a kilojoule (calorie) saving and assist weight loss strategies.

Splenda® has been used in many recipes in this book. It provides negligible kilojoules (calories) and will not adversely affect blood glucose values. People who are not trying to lose weight may find they can use sugar in small amounts.

If the recipe has low-fat ingredients and low-fat preparation methods, and the use of a low-joule (low-calorie) sweetener results in a lower blood glucose reading than when sweetened with sugar, then the low-joule (low-calorie) sweetener is preferable to use.

Saturated fats

The recipes help minimise saturated fats. This is important to improve blood glucose control, to control blood fats such as cholesterol and triglycerides, and because excess fat in the diet is readily stored as fat and thus will contribute to obesity. Fat is the most energy-rich of all nutrients.

Some fat is necessary for health and it is preferable that the small amounts used are of the healthier unsaturated fats, such as canola or olive oil. The recipes show that small amounts of fat can be used judiciously to add to the flavour of foods, which is important for keeping healthy food tasting great.

Jenny Holliday APD
Consultant Dietitian
Jenny Holliday Nutrition Solutions Pty Ltd

Contents

• •

Recipes

*Each recipe indicates whether the dish contains milk or meat, or if it is
pareve (neutral) and can be eaten with either milk or meat.*

Preface

My credentials for compiling *The Jewish Diabetes Cookbook* are that I am Jewish and that I have diabetes. I therefore know only too well how difficult it is to combine the specialised dietary needs of each of these groups

The recipes have been made as easy as possible, and simple, easily obtained ingredients have been used throughout. One of the aims of this book is to make cooking easier. It shows that meals can be both interesting and suitable for all members of the family. Diabetes is prevalent in many ethnic groups but not all have special dietary laws. Although there are many cookbooks for people with diabetes—and even more of Jewish cooking— there are none, that I've been able to find, which cater for both. *The Jewish Diabetes Cookbook* will, I hope, fill this gap.

I wrote this cookbook on and off for a period of about four years. As I tested, adapted and cooked, it became clear that the book would also be useful for anyone on a low-cholesterol diet and anyone who wants to lose weight. The result is a collection of recipes, which will prove that juggling a diabetes diet with a kosher diet need not be tedious.

Only some of the recipes, such as those in the Herring and Passover sections, are traditional Jewish recipes. So, even though I only used ingredients approved by the NSW Kashrut Authority, you don't have to be Jewish to use and enjoy this book. For this reason I have not specified brand names but I have checked that all of the ingredients are available in a kosher form.

Because I am not a dietitian, I am not qualified to give anyone advice on how to manage their diabetes and diet. All I have attempted to do here is to show that people with diabetes do not need special foods.

The Glycaemic Index has not been used in *The Jewish Diabetes Cookbook*. The serves are sufficient for one portion (15g carbohydrate) only. Therefore people with diabetes should adjust their meal according to the needs of their own diet.

I advise everyone who uses this book to invest in a small, good electronic scale. I also advise the purchase of a set of metric (imperial) cup and spoon measures, as these too are invaluable aids to accuracy.

In regard to the sugar content of the recipes, Splenda® has been used as a substitute in all recipes except those for Passover, where small amounts of sugar have been used instead. Splenda® is not suitable for this festival as corn is used in its manufacture. Other sugar substitutes are labelled 'Not for use in cooking', so many Passover cakes, sweets and desserts had to be omitted. However, Splenda® can be successfully used in most Passover recipes at any other time. These were not tested.

No recipes for Jewish festivals, other than Passover, have been included because their fat and sugar content are too high for people with diabetes. Judicious consumption of the foods for these festivals on special occasions is left to the reader's judgement.

Although current recommendations suggest that people with diabetes can have small amounts of sugar and honey in their diet, I chose not to include them.

The recipes in *The Jewish Diabetes Cookbook* came from countless sources, friends and family. All ingredients were carefully weighed and measured (in metric) to ensure the accuracy of the recipes. All recipes were tested, and my ever-patient family tasted the finished products. The result will, I hope, be acceptable to all people with diabetes, Jewish or not.

I welcome comments and suggestions and invite you to email me at: rachi@ozemail.com.au

Acknowledgments

This book would not have been possible without the invaluable help of Daphne Rawicz, my cousin in Johannesburg, South Africa. She jumped at the chance of helping with the recipes because she is a dedicated cook and the project interested her. She spent many hours in her kitchen weighing, testing and tasting and we corresponded several times a week for many months via email, sharing family recipes, swapping others and discussing ideas for changes in them and the layout. The finished product is a tribute to her enthusiasm and generosity.

I am indebted to Ms Kate Wallis, Marketing Manager of J & J Pacific, for supplying huge quantities of Splenda®, which was used instead of sugar in all the recipes except those for the Passover. Kate's encouragement and generous help with this project right from the start have been invaluable.

J & J Pacific also provided the services of an excellent dietitian, Ms Jenny Holliday, APD, who did the food analyses for all the recipes. I thank Jenny for her contribution and for her important Foreword.

I am especially indebted to my husband, Rachi, who shared his computer knowledge and expertise in formatting, designing and producing. Without his help and useful comments this book may never have been produced.

I hope that this book will enhance the lives of all Jewish people with diabetes and ease the problems of weaving a diet for diabetes with a Jewish one.

Any errors in *The Jewish Diabetes Cookbook* are mine alone and do not in any way reflect upon the assistance given to me by anyone else.

A Brief History of Jewish Cooking

The Jewish tradition of hospitality began 4000 years ago when Abraham welcomed three strangers into his tent (Genesis 18:1-8). Since then it has been incorporated into Jewish belief and faith. During this time Jews have been guests, not always welcome, in diverse countries for varying lengths of time. These sojourns in host countries are known as the Diaspora. During the centuries of wanderings, many aspects of Jewish life, including the cuisine, benefited from contact with these different cultures. Jewish cooking reflects the inventiveness of women as they adapted local ingredients and methods of cooking to the laws of kashrut while struggling to feed their families during the all-too-often times of poverty and oppression.

Jews fall into two broad, often overlapping, groups: Ashkenazic and Sephardic. Ashkenazic Jews come from central and eastern Europe: Austria, Germany, Hungary, Poland and Russia. Sephardic Jews come from Spain, Portugal and the Middle East. Now Jews live in every country of the world such as Australia, New Zealand, South Africa, England, America, China, India, Europe and many others. Thus, although the cuisine of each group is distinctive, today's rapidly changing borders and better communications mean this distinctiveness is diminishing.

Since the establishment of the State of Israel in May 1948, Jews from many different countries have sought refuge there, and Jewish cooking has undergone a minor revolution. Methods of cooking from every corner of the world are 'mixed and matched' to create new, mouth-watering dishes using the large variety of fresh produce available from the orchards and market gardens of the once arid desert.

Many Jews, however, still live in the Diaspora and their food, as that of their ancestors, draws on the ingredients and methods of their adopted countries.

Thus, Jewish cooking today reflects the differences and changes of Jewish history, and there are, therefore, no real, distinctively Jewish recipes. Although there are traditional dishes for all the festivals, even these differ depending on whether they are Ashkenazic or Sephardic and in what country they are being cooked. The only common point they have is their adherence to the laws of kashrut.

These laws are complex but, broadly speaking, mixing milk and meat products and the consumption of the meat of animals that do not have cloven hooves and chew their cud and of fish that do not have scales or gills is forbidden. Thus, shellfish and meat from pigs and certain other animals are forbidden. Kashrut also precludes the consumption of blood, which is why only the meat of animals slaughtered in the prescribed manner and drained of blood by salting is allowed and why eggs with bloodspots are always discarded.

The recipes in *The Jewish Diabetes Cookbook* follow the basic laws of kashrut (keeping kosher), in that milk and meat are not used together and foods forbidden to Jews are not included in any recipe. Some recipes are listed as 'pareve', which means that they are neutral and can be eaten with either milk or meat.

The Kosher Authority of New South Wales' lists of approved products have been consulted for all the recipes, and all care has been taken to ensure that only approved products were used when recipes were tested. No brand names were used.

No claim is made, however, that these recipes fulfil all kashrut requirements. Please consult the Kosher Authority nearest to you or a rabbi if you have any questions or doubts.

Key to Abbreviations

1 exchange = 15 g of carbohydrates
1 oz = 28.4 g (Rounded to 30 g)
1 calorie = 4.18 kilojoules

P = protein
CHO= carbohydrate
F = fat
KJ= kilojoules
C = calories

5-10 g CHO= ½ exchange
11-19 g CHO= 1 exchange
20-25 g CHO= 1.5 exchanges
26-34 g CHO= 2 exchanges
35-40 g CHO= 2.5 exchanges
41-49 g CHO= 3 exchanges

Splenda® Brand Sweetener, produced by Johnson & Johnson, is the name of the low joule sweetening ingredient known as Sucralose. Sucralose is produced from sugar (sucrose) by a patented process. It is inert in the body (it is not metabolised) and thus provides no kilojoules.

Splenda® is used in commercial products displaying the Splenda® logo, and is available in granular form, which is used spoon for spoon the same as sugar, and in tablets.

Sucralose has no effect on blood sugar or insulin levels. This is because Sucralose is not recognised by the body as a carbohydrate. Even in large amounts, Sucralose has no joules.

Splenda® is made from sugar and tastes like sugar without sugar's joules. It can be used in place of sugar in virtually all types of foods resulting in lower joule, lower sugar products that can be used as part of a healthy diet. For the person with diabetes, this means that foods typically avoided because of high sugar content may now be prepared with Splenda® and enjoyed. Splenda® can even be used to replace sugar in baking and cooking without losing its sweet sugar-like taste.

Because of these unique properties, Splenda®, unlike other low joule sweeteners, can be added to recipes prior to baking, stewing or boiling, just like sugar. Following a recipe is just like following regular recipes.

Information supplied by Johnson & Johnson Pacific, Stephen Road, Botany NSW AUSTRALIA 2019. For further information on Splenda® contact your nearest Johnson & Johnson office.

If Splenda® is not available in your region, please contact your dietitian or health practitioner for an alternative.

Cakes and Biscuits (Cookies)

Ann's Apple Pie (*milk*)

Pikelets (*pareve*)

Fruit Buns (*milk*)

Marian's Chocolate Cake (*pareve*)

Sharon's Farfel Slice (*pareve*)

Poppyseed Biscuits (Cookies) (*pareve*)

Scones (*milk*)

Ann's Apple Pie *(milk)*

Ingredients

150 g (5 oz) self-raising flour

15 g (½ oz) Splenda®

125 g (4 oz) margarine

50 ml (1 ½ fl oz) low-fat milk

2 eggs

400 g (13 oz) can pie apples

Method

- Blend all ingredients, except apples, together well
- Place dough into lightly oiled pie dish
- Press apple into dough
- Sprinkle with mixture of cinnamon and Splenda® if desired
- Bake in middle of oven at 180°C (350°F) for 40 minutes

Serves 9
Approximate carbohydrate value per serve: 1 exchange
Per serve: P—3.0 g; F—12.6 g; CHO—15.6 g; KJ—785 (C—188)

Pikelets *(pareve)*

Ingredients

2 eggs
2 rounded teaspoons Splenda®
100 ml (3 fl oz) water
140 g (4 ⅔ oz) flour
2 rounded teaspoons baking powder
Pinch of salt

Method

- Sift flour and baking flour
- Beat eggs well with Splenda® till thick
- Add water and sifted flour and baking powder alternately beating well after each addition
- Oil a pan very lightly and heat
- Drop tablespoonfuls batter onto hot pan
- When it bubbles, turn pikelets over with a spatula

Yields 14 pikelets
Approximate carbohydrate value per pikelet: ½ exchange
Per pikelet: P—1.8 g; F—0.8 g; CHO—6.6 g; KJ—170 (C—41)

Fruit Buns *(milk)*

Ingredients

2 ¼ cups (11 oz) flour

½ teaspoon salt

4 teaspoons baking powder

40 g (1 ⅓ oz) margarine

2 level tablespoons Splenda®

130 g (4 ⅓ oz) mixed fruit or sultanas

1 egg

100 ml (3 fl oz) low-fat milk

Method

- Whisk egg and milk
- Mix dry ingredients
- Rub margarine into dry ingredients until mixture resembles breadcrumbs
- Add fruit and then egg and milk
- Roll into balls and place on a lightly greased baking tray
- Bake at 220°C (430°F) for 12-15 minutes

Serves 12
Approximate carbohydrate value per bun: 2 exchanges
Per serve: P—3.7 g; F—3.5 g; CHO—27.6 g; KJ—660 (C—158)

Marian's Chocolate Cake *(pareve)*

● ●

Ingredients

4 eggs, separated

1 cup (5 oz) flour

2 teaspoons baking powder

14 g (½ oz) cocoa

24 ml (1 fl oz) oil

¾ cup (½ oz) Splenda®

¼ cup (1 fl oz) boiling water

½ teaspoon vanilla essence

Method

- Beat egg whites well and put into fridge
- Cream Splenda® and egg yolks
- Dissolve cocoa in boiling water
- Add flour and cocoa to yolk mixture
- Add oil and blend
- Sprinkle baking powder on top and beat in
- Fold in egg whites
- Bake in two 20 cm (8 in) sandwich tins at 190°C (380°F) for about 20 minutes
- When cool sandwich together with low-joule (low-calorie) jam

Serves 8
Approximate carbohydrate value per slice: 1 exchange
Per serve: P—5.4 g; F—6.0 g; CHO—16.9 g; KJ—600 (C—143)

Sharon's Farfel Slice *(pareve)*

Ingredients

120 g (4 oz) margarine

1 tablespoon Splenda®

Lemon essence

2 tablespoons oil

1 egg

2 cups (10 oz) flour

Pinch of salt

2 teaspoons baking powder

2 tablespoons low-joule (low-calorie) jam

Method

- Cream margarine and Splenda®
- Add essence and mix
- Mix oil and egg together and add to creamed mixture
- Add flour and salt but note that not all flour is always used
- Mix well and then add baking powder
- Halve mixture and line small Swiss roll tin with one half
- Spread with jam
- Grate remaining dough over jam
- Bake at 190°C (380°F) for about 30 minutes
- Cut into squares while warm

Serves 24
Approximate carbohydrate value per slice: ½ exchange
Per serve: P—1.3 g; F—6.0 g; CHO—8.0 g; KJ—380 (C—91)

Poppyseed Biscuits (Cookies)

(pareve)

● ●

Ingredients

> 1 cup (5 oz) flour
>
> ¼ teaspoon bicarbonate of soda
>
> ¼ teaspoon salt
>
> 125 g (4 oz) margarine
>
> 2 ½ tablespoons Splenda®
>
> 1 egg
>
> 2 tablespoons poppy seeds
>
> ¾ teaspoon vanilla essence

Method

- Sift dry ingredients
- Cream margarine and Splenda®
- Add other ingredients and beat well
- Put onto greased baking tray in teaspoonsful
- Bake at 175°C (340°F) for 15-20 minutes

Yields approximately 24 biscuits
Approximate carbohydrate value per 2 Biscuits: ½ exchange
Per biscuit: P—1.0 g; F—4.5 g; CHO—4.0 g; KJ—255 (C—61)

Scones *(milk)*

Ingredients

2 cups (10 oz) flour

4 teaspoons baking powder

1 tablespoon Splenda®

Pinch of salt

90 g (3 oz) margarine

200 g (7 oz) low-fat plain yoghurt

1 beaten egg

Method

- Sift dry ingredients
- Mix margarine with dry ingredients in mixer till it resembles fine breadcrumbs
- Add yoghurt and egg
- Spoon into greased patty tins
- Bake at 200°C (400°F) for 15-16 minutes

Yields 12 scones
Approximate carbohydrate value per scone: 1 exchange
Per scone: P—4.0 g; F—6.9 g; CHO—16.2 g; KJ—600 (C—144)

Desserts

Marcelle Pudding (*milk*)

Rice Custard (*milk*)

Ricotta Fruit Cup (*milk*)

Chocolate Sauce (*pareve*)

Stewed Apples (*pareve*)

Marcelle Pudding *(milk)*

Ingredients

60 g (2 oz) margarine

2 cups (10 oz) self-raising flour

1 cup (¾ oz) Splenda®

250 ml (8 fl oz) low-fat milk

Pinch of salt

Optional: 425 g (14 oz) tin fruit in natural juice,
    drained or 1 tin pie apples or apricots

Method

• Melt margarine in bottom of 20 cm (8 in) square tin
• Mix all ingredients together except fruit
• Add fruit if desired and put into tin
• Bake at 190°C (380°F) for about 35 minutes

Serves 16
Approximate carbohydrate value per serve (no fruit): 1 exchange
Approximate carbohydrate value per serve (with fruit): 1 exchange
Per serve (no fruit): P—2.1g; F—3.3 g; CHO—12.6 g; KJ—370 (C—88)
Per serve (with fruit): P—2.1 g; F—3.3 g; CHO—15 g; KJ—410
(C—98)

Rice Custard *(milk)*

Ingredients

1 ¼ cups (6 oz) cooked rice

2 eggs

450 ml (15 fl oz) low-fat milk

1 teaspoon vanilla essence or 1 tablespoon low-joule
(low-calorie) jam

1 teaspoon Splenda®

Nutmeg

20 g (⅔ oz) sultanas (optional)

Method

- Mix rice, eggs, milk, Splenda® and vanilla
- Put in suitable oven or microwave dish
- Sprinkle with nutmeg
- Bake at 175°C (350°F) for 30 minutes or until set
- Can be microwaved for 7-10 minutes on high

Serves 4
Approximate carbohydrate value per serve without sultanas:
1.5 exchanges
Approximate carbohydrate value per serve with sultanas: 2 exchanges

Per serve (no sultanas): P—8.5 g; F—2.7 g; CHO—22.6 g; KJ—620
(C—148)
Per serve (with sultanas): P—8.5 g; F—2.7 g; CHO 26.0 g; KJ—685
(C—164)

Ricotta Fruit Cup *(milk)*

Ingredients

500 g (1 lb 1 oz) ricotta cheese
(low-fat is not kosher)
1 punnet strawberries
2 tablespoons Splenda®

Method

- Clean, hull and halve strawberries
- Process ricotta till smooth
- Add other ingredients and process till smooth
- Put into dessert cups
- Chill

Note: Very good with mango but not kiwifruit

Serves 6
Approximate carbohydrate value per serve: negligible
Per serve: P—9.4 g; F—7.3 g; CHO—3.5 g; KJ—485 (C—116)

Chocolate Sauce *(pareve)*

● ●

Ingredients

80 g (2 ½ oz) cocoa (use 60 g/2 oz for a
   sweeter sauce)

1 ½ cups (1 oz) Splenda®

Pinch of salt

425 ml (14 fl oz) boiling water

1 teaspoon vanilla essence

Method

- Sift cocoa, Splenda® and salt into a saucepan
- Add the boiling water and stir well
- Bring to the boil whisking all the time
- Stop whisking and boil for exactly one minute
- Remove from heat and add essence
- Cool slightly
- Pour into a jar with a tightly fitting lid
- Seal and cool completely

Can be used hot or cold
Will keep for about one month in the fridge
Cocoa is not recommended in large amounts due to the fat
content

Yields 425 ml (14 fl oz)
Serves 8 x 60 ml (2 fl oz) serves
Approximate carbohydrate value: negligible in small quantities; 60 ml (2 fl
oz) serve = ½ exchange
Per serve: P—2.0 g; F—1.4 g; CHO—6.7 g; KJ—200 (C—48)

Stewed Apples *(pareve)*

Ingredients

1 kg (2 lb 2 oz) green apples

Just under ½ cup (⅓ oz) Splenda®

30 g (1 oz) sultanas (optional)

50 ml (1 ½ fl oz) water

Method

- Peel and cut apples into suitably sized pieces
- Place in pot
- Add other ingredients
- Cook on high on top of stove till it boils then switch plate off
- Let stand on hotplate for a little while, then remove
- Cool and then refrigerate

Note: Can be microwaved on high for 8-10 minutes but use only 25 ml (1 fl oz) water

Serves 6
Approximate carbohydrate value per serve: 1.5 exchanges
Approximate carbohydrate value per serve with sultanas: 2 exchanges
Per serve (no sultanas): P—0.5 g; F—0 g; CHO—19.6 g; KJ—333 (C—80)
Per serve (with sultanas): P—0.6 g; F—0 g; CHO—23.3 g; KJ—397 (C—95)

Extras

Marinated Mushrooms (*pareve*)

Eggplant (Aubergine) Pâté (*pareve*)

Half-pickled Cucumbers (*pareve*)

Tamm (*pareve*)

Hummus (*pareve*)

Marinated Mushrooms *(pareve)*

Ingredients

250 g (8 oz) medium white mushrooms

300 ml (10 fl oz) water

A little lemon juice

Method

- Peel mushrooms and cut in half
- Bring water and lemon juice to boil
- Add mushrooms and simmer for 3 minutes
- Drain well and place in bowl

Marinade ingredients

75 ml (2 ½ fl oz) vinegar

1 tablespoon olive oil

1 clove garlic, crushed

½ teaspoon salt

⅛ teaspoon thyme

Pinch of coriander

A few peppercorns and bay leaves

Method

- Bring marinade to the boil
- Immediately pour over the drained mushrooms
- Serve chilled

Serves 4
Approximate carbohydrate value per serve: negligible
Per serve: P—2.3 g; F—5.2 g; CHO—1.0 g; KJ—250 (C—60)

Eggplant (Aubergine) Pâté *(pareve)*

● ●

Ingredients

1 large eggplant (aubergine), about 300 g (10 oz)

2-3 teaspoons lemon juice

¼ teaspoon salt

1 small onion (about 40 g/1 ⅓ oz) chopped

A little paprika

Pepper to taste

Method

- Boil eggplants till soft or microwave for at least 4 minutes
- Peel and discard peel
- Mash eggplant (aubergine) with all other ingredients or blend in processor
- Season to taste
- Serve well chilled

Serves 6
Approximate carbohydrate value per serve: negligible
Per serve: P—0.7g; F—0.2 g; CHO—1.6 g; KJ—45 (C—11)

Half-pickled Cucumbers *(pareve)*

Ingredients

500 g (1 lb 1 oz) Lebanese cucumbers

24 peppercorns

10 bay leaves

4 cloves garlic, peeled and halved

200 ml (7 fl oz) white vinegar

600 ml (20 fl oz) water

6 teaspoons Splenda®

1 tablespoon salt

Method

- Slice the washed but unpeeled cucumbers into ½ cm (¼ in) slices
- Place in a large jar with peppercorns, bay leaves and garlic
- Bring the remaining ingredients to the boil and cook for a few minutes
- Allow to cool
- Pour over cucumbers and refrigerate for at least 12 hours before serving

Serves 5
Approximate carbohydrate value per serve: negligible
Per serve: P—0.7 g; F—0.2 g; CHO—2.9 g; KJ—95 (C—23)

Tamm *(pareve)*

• •

Ingredients

240 g (8 oz) cabbage

190 g (6 oz) green apple

100 g (3 ⅓ oz) onion

1 tablespoon oil

Method

- Shred cabbage, grate apple and chop onion
- Stir-fry together in a little oil till golden brown
- Serve as an accompaniment to fried fish or steak

Serves 4
Approximate carbohydrate value per serve: ½ Exchange, negligible in small quantities
Per serve: P—1.5 g; F—5.1 g; CHO—7.0 g; KJ—330 (C—79)

Hummus *(pareve)*

● ●

Ingredients

320 g (11 oz) tin chickpeas

75 g (2 ½ oz) tahini

2 or more tablespoons lemon juice,
    according to taste

1-2 large cloves garlic, according to taste,
    finely crushed

Method

- Mix all ingredients together very well
- Will keep in fridge for a few days

Serves 10
Approximate carbohydrate value per serve: negligible
Per serve: P—4.6 g; F—10.0 g; CHO—3.2 g; KJ—500 (C—120)

Fish

Pickled Curried Fish (*pareve*)

Gefilte Fish (*pareve*)

Salmon Mayonnaise (*milk*)

Ada's Fishcakes (*pareve*)

Curried Tuna (*pareve*)

Salade Nicoise (*pareve*)

Mock Crayfish (*pareve*)

Pickled Curried Fish *(pareve)*

Ingredients

1 kg (2 lb 2 oz) firm white fish

¼ cup (1 oz) flour

Salt and pepper

1 ½ tablespoons oil for frying

Method

- Shake pieces of fish in a plastic bag with the flour and seasoning
- Fry fish until done
- Drain and cool

Sauce Ingredients

180 g (6 oz) sliced onions

250 ml (8 fl oz) water

1 tablespoon Splenda®

350 ml (12 fl oz) vinegar

1 ½ tablespoons curry powder
(adjust according to taste)

2 teaspoons cornflour (cornstarch)

12 peppercorns and 6 bay leaves

Method

- Boil the onions, water, peppercorns and bay leaves
- Mix curry powder, Splenda® and cornflour (cornstarch) to a paste with a little vinegar
- Add the remaining vinegar
- Pour this mixture into the boiling onions and cook until the onions are soft
- Layer fish and onions and then pour the liquid over
- Cover and refrigerate
- Ready in 1-2 days

Note: Also suitable for fishcakes

Serves at least 6
Approximate carbohydrate value per serve: ½ exchange
Per serve: P—36.2 g; F—9.6 g; CHO—7.4 g; KJ—1130 (C—270)

Gefilte Fish *(pareve)*

● ●

Ingredients

400 g (13 oz) firm white fish

150 g (5 oz) onion

200 g (7 oz) carrots

1 egg

Parsley

Salt and pepper

A few shakes of turmeric

Method

- Skin fish if necessary but retain skin
- Boil 100 g (3 ½ oz) onion, 100 g (3 ½ oz) carrot, turmeric and fish skin in a large pot
- Mince or process fish and remaining onion and carrot together
- Form into balls and add to boiling water
- Cook for about 10 minutes after they rise to the top of the pot
- Remove with a slotted spoon and place in a suitable dish
- Decorate each fish ball with a slice of carrot
- Add a little broth to the dish and cover
- Chill well

Will keep for a couple of days

Yields 8 balls
Approximate carbohydrate value per serve: negligible
Per serve: P—15.5 g; F—2.4 g; CHO—0.5 g; KJ—360 (C—86)

Salmon Mayonnaise *(milk)*

Ingredients

415 g (14 oz) tin salmon

40 g (1 ⅓ oz) pickled cucumbers

6 olives

2 hard-boiled eggs

3 shallots or a small amount of onion, chopped

Salt and pepper to taste

50 ml (1 ½ fl oz) light mayonnaise or mayonnaise and
   light yoghurt mixed

Dash of lemon juice to taste

Method

- Drain salmon and reserve liquid
- Dice cucumbers, olives and eggs
- Add salmon liquid to mayonnaise
- Season to taste
- Break up salmon with a fork
- Combine with other ingredients
- Chill

Serves 3
Approximate carbohydrate value per serve: ¼ exchange
Per serve: P—31.1g; F—21.8 g; CHO—4.3 g; KJ—1410 (C—337)

Ada's Fishcakes *(pareve)*

● ●

Ingredients

500 g (1 lb 1 oz) white fish

40 g (1 ⅓ oz) onion

70 g (2 oz) carrot

1 egg

Salt and pepper to taste

50 ml (1 ½ fl oz) olive oil

100 ml (3 fl oz) iced water

Parsley can be added to recipe if desired

Method

- Mince fish, onion and carrot
- Add egg and seasoning and begin mixing in electric mixer
- Slowly add oil and water and beat well till mixture is light and fluffy (about 10-15 minutes)
- Shape into rissoles with wet hands
- Fry in shallow oil till brown on both sides
- Drain on paper towels
- Freezes well

Yields 12 fishcakes
Approximate carbohydrate value per fishcake: negligible
Per serve: P—9.3 g; F—5.8 g; CHO—0.5 g; KJ—380 (C—91)

Curried Tuna *(pareve)*

Ingredients

150 g (5 oz) onion, chopped

140 g (4 ⅔ oz) celery, chopped

425 g (14 oz) tin tuna in brine, undrained

240 g (8 oz) potato, grated

125 g (4 oz) carrot, grated

1 clove garlic, chopped or crushed

1 tablespoon curry powder or more as desired

1 tablespoon olive oil

Method

- Sauté onions and celery in the oil
- Add other ingredients and cook, stirring occasionally, until vegetables are done

Serves 3
Approximate carbohydrate value per serve: 1 exchange
Per serve: P—26.0 g; F—4.8 g; CHO—16.7 g; KJ—920 (C—220)

Salade Nicoise *(pareve)*

Ingredients

150 g (5 oz) tomatoes, cut into eighths

30 g (1 oz) sliced onions or shallots

35 g (1 oz) sliced capsicum

60 g (2 oz) sliced radishes

185 g (6 oz) tin tuna in brine, drained and diced

25 g (1 oz) anchovies, drained and cut into pieces

2 hard-boiled eggs, cut into eighths

4 olives, sliced or halved

Method

- Mix all ingredients together in a salad bowl

Dressing Ingredients

20 ml (⅔ fl oz) vinegar or lemon juice

30 ml (1 fl oz) olive oil

¼ teaspoon basil leaves

Salt and pepper to taste

Method

- Mix together well
- Pour over salad and mix well
- Chill
- Serve on a bed of lettuce if desired

Serves 3
Approximate carbohydrate value per serve: negligible
Per serve: P—16.9 g; F—18.7 g; CHO—2.6 g; KJ—1030 (C—246)

Mock Crayfish *(pareve)*

● ●

Ingredients

400 g (13 oz) firm white fish

Salt and pepper to taste

50 g (1 ½ oz) onion

2 bay leaves

4 peppercorns

Water to almost cover

Method

- Simmer ingredients together for about 10 minutes
- Remove fish from pot and remove skin if necessary
- Cool in fridge till fish is firm
- Flake fish

Sauce Ingredients

30 g (1 oz) onion, finely chopped

100 ml (3 oz) tomato puree

100 ml (3 oz) light mayonnaise

½ teaspoon Worcestershire sauce

Method

- Mix sauce ingredients together well
- Pour over flaked fish and mix well
- Chill

Serves 4
Approximate carbohydrate value per serve: ¼ exchange
Per serve: P—10.8 g; F—4.1 g; CHO—4.1 g; KJ—400 (C—96)

Herring

Chopped Herring (*pareve*)

Russian Herring (*milk*)

Danish Herring (*pareve*)

Mustard Herring (*milk*)

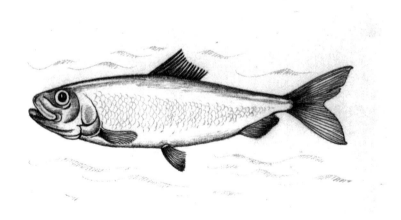

Chopped Herring *(pareve)*

· ·

Ingredients

8 matjes herring fillets, rinsed and drained

1 medium onion

2 medium green or red apples

2 slices of white bread

2 hard-boiled eggs

Vinegar, salt and pepper to taste

Splenda® to taste

Method

- Mince or process herring, onion, apples, bread and eggs together
- Add a little Splenda® to taste if required
- Will keep in an airtight jar in fridge for several weeks

Serves 8
Approximate carbohydrate value per serve: 1 exchange
Per serve: P—9.7 g; F—10.5 g; CHO—12.6 g; KJ—770 (C—184)

Russian Herring *(milk)*

Ingredients

6 matjes herring fillets, rinsed, drained and cut into
bite-sized pieces

240 g (8 oz) potatoes, cooked, peeled and sliced

2 hard-boiled eggs, sliced

125 ml (4 fl oz) light mayonnaise and low-fat
yoghurt mixed together

60 g (2 oz) cooked peas

Cherry tomatoes or tomato wedges

Cucumber slices

Salt and pepper to taste

Method

• Mix all ingredients together and chill

Serves 10
Approximate carbohydrate values per serve: ½ exchange
Per serve: P—7.0 g; F—7.7 g; CHO—8.3 g; KJ—550 (C—130)

Danish Herring *(pareve)*

Ingredients

250 g (8 oz) matjes herring fillets, rinsed and drained

120 g (4 oz) apple, diced

150 g (5 oz) onion, chopped

2 tablespoons vinegar

2 tablespoons water

8 tablespoons tomato puree

2 tablespoons Splenda®

Method

- Cut herring into suitably sized pieces
- Add apples and onion and combine well
- Mix liquids and Splenda® well
- Pour over herring and mix gently
- Store in the refrigerator for two days before serving

Serves 10
Approximate carbohydrate value per serve: ½ exchange
Per serve: P—4.0 g; F—4.5 g; CHO—5.0 g; KJ—330 (C—79)

Mustard Herring *(milk)*

Ingredients

250 g (8 oz) matjes herring fillets, rinsed, drained
and cut into bite-sized pieces

15 g (½ oz) mild made mustard

30 ml (1 fl oz) olive oil

60 g (2 oz) low-fat plain yoghurt

1 tablespoon Splenda®

30 g (1 oz) pickled or fresh cucumber, diced

Method

- Add cucumber to herring in a bowl
- Mix other ingredients well and add to herring and cucumbers
- Adjust mustard and Splenda® as desired
- Store in fridge for 24 hours before serving

Serves 10
Approximate carbohydrate value per serve: negligible
Per serve: P—4.0 g; F—7.6 g; CHO—2.7 g; KJ—400 (C—96)

Meat

Chopped Liver (*Pâté*)

Shashlik (*Kebabs*)

Eastern Meatballs

Frikkadels (*Hamburgers*)

Bolognaise

Chicken Liver à la Grecque

Beef Rachi

Stuffed Capsicum

Chopped Liver *(Pâté)*

Ingredients

500 g (1 lb 1 oz) chicken or beef liver

180 g (6 oz) onion, peeled and roughly chopped

A little olive oil

3 hard-boiled eggs

Salt and pepper to taste

Method

- Clean and trim the liver
- Grill under a hot grill or fry in a little oil until well done
- Fry the onions in the oil till brown
- Process all ingredients till blended
- Add a little extra oil if pâté seems too dry
- Add seasoning

Serves 10

Approximate carbohydrate value per serve: negligible

Per serve: P—12.1 g; F—7.8 g; CHO—2.2 g; KJ—530 (C—127)

Shashlik *(Kebabs)*

● ●

Ingredients

500 g (1 lb 1 oz) lean beef or lamb cut into
bite-sized cubes

2 cloves garlic, crushed

30 ml (1 fl oz) olive oil

15 ml (½ fl oz) lemon juice

1 ½ teaspoons dried oregano

Salt and pepper to taste

Method

- Marinate meat in oil, seasoning and garlic for about 30 minutes
- Put meat on skewers
- Grill on the barbecue or in the stove grill till well done

Variations

Liver cubes, onions, capsicum, cherry tomatoes and/or button mushrooms may be put on the skewers with the meat.

Serves 8
Approximate carbohydrate value per serve: negligible
Per serve: P—13.5 g; F—6.4 g; CHO—0 g; KJ—470 (C—112)

Eastern Meatballs

Ingredients

500 g (1 lb 1 oz) lean mince

30 g (1 oz) bread

1 egg

½ teaspoon mustard powder or 1 teaspoon made-up
mustard of choice

½ teaspoon garlic powder or 1 small clove garlic,
crushed

½ teaspoon powdered ginger

15 ml (½ fl oz) oil for frying

2 tablespoons cornflour (cornstarch)

Method

- Moisten bread and squeeze out
- Mix all ingredients except oil and cornflour together well
- Form into 10 balls
- Roll lightly in cornflour and shake off excess
- Brown well in the oil in a pan
- Remove meatballs and drain off excess oil

Sauce Ingredients

3 ½ tablespoons Splenda®

75 ml (2 ½ fl oz) soy sauce

75 ml (2 ½ fl oz) dry sherry

75 ml (2 ½ fl oz) white vinegar

Method

- Mix together and pour into pan
- Add meatballs and cook till nicely glazed and sauce has thickened

Serves 4

Approximate carbohydrate value per serve: ½ exchange

Per serve: P—30.2 g; F—10.5 g; CHO—9.8 g; KJ—1160 (C—280)

Frikkadels *(Hamburgers)*

Ingredients

1 kg (2 lb 2 oz) lean mince

30 g (1 oz) onion, chopped

30 g (1 oz) breadcrumbs

100 ml (3 fl oz) water

1 egg

Salt and pepper to taste

15 g (½ oz) chopped fresh parsley, or 1 teaspoon
dried parsley

Method

- Mix all ingredients together well
- Form into patties
- Fry in a little oil till well done on both sides

Serves 8
Approximate carbohydrate value per patty: negligible
Per serve: P—28.0 g; F—6.0 g; CHO—2.0 g; KJ—730 (C—175)

Bolognaise

● ●

Ingredients

1 kg (2 lb 2 oz) lean mince

1 medium onion, roughly chopped

1 large clove garlic, roughly chopped

3 bay leaves

4-6 peppercorns

1 heaped teaspoon each of oregano, paprika, tarragon, coriander, mixed herbs (leaves, not ground)

250 ml (8 fl oz) tomato puree

125 ml (4 fl oz) red wine

1 tablespoon olive oil

Method

- Brown spices, onion and garlic in oil in a large pot
- Add meat and brown
- Add puree and wine
- Simmer till sauce is reduced and thick, stirring occasionally.

Serves 8
Approximate carbohydrate value per serve: negligible
Per serve: P—27.7 g; F—7.8 g; CHO—2.5 g; KJ—850 (C—203)

Chicken Liver à la Grecque

Ingredients

1 ½ tablespoons olive oil

60 g (2 oz) onion, chopped

1 medium clove garlic, chopped

60 g (2 oz) capsicum, chopped

500 g (1 lb 1 oz) chicken livers

150 g (5 oz) cooked chicken cut into bite-sized pieces (optional)

425 g (14 oz) tin mushrooms, drained but reserve about 125 ml (4 fl oz) liquid

360 g (12 oz) cooked rice

12 olives, black, green or stuffed, cut up a little

A couple of squeezes lemon juice

Method

- Heat oil in large pan and lightly brown onions, garlic and capsicum on medium heat
- Add trimmed livers and cook till done through
- If adding chicken, add now and heat thoroughly
- Add mushrooms and rice and stir well, add olives and heat well
- Add some of reserved mushroom liquid only if mixture seems too dry
- Add lemon juice and stir well

Serves 6
Approximate carbohydrate value per serve: 1.5 exchanges
Per serve: P—20.2 g; F—13.1 g; CHO—20.8 g; KJ—1180 (C—282)

Beef Rachi

Ingredients

1 kg (2 lb 2 oz) scotch fillet cut into strips

260 g (9 oz) spinach, washed and torn into
small pieces

150 g (5 oz) mushrooms, peeled and sliced thinly

3 tablespoons soy sauce

2 heaped teaspoons cornflour (cornstarch)

1 heaped teaspoon mustard powder

Method

- Cook spinach for a few minutes till just done and drain
- Blend soy sauce, cornflour and mustard well
- Add to meat ensuring that all pieces are covered
- Stand for about 30 minutes
- Stir-fry meat in a little oil in a large frying pan or wok until seared
- Add spinach and mushrooms and cover pan
- Simmer, stirring occasionally, until meat is cooked through

Serves 8
Approximate carbohydrate value per serve: negligible
Per serve: P—30.0 g; F—8.7 g; CHO—1.6 g; KJ—860 (C—206)

Stuffed Capsicum

Ingredients

1 tablespoon olive oil

100 g (3 ⅓ oz) onion, chopped

1 large clove garlic, chopped

750 g (1 lb 9 oz) lean mince

400 g (13 oz) fresh tomatoes, roughly chopped

200 g (7 oz) mushrooms, sliced

Salt and pepper to taste

100 g (3 ⅓ oz) tomato paste

1 tablespoon dried basil

6 large capsicums, red or green

Method

- In a large pot, fry onion, garlic and meat in oil till brown and well separated
- Drain off any liquid
- Add tomatoes and mushrooms and fry till tender
- Add salt, pepper, tomato paste and basil and cook on low till not sloppy
- Cut off tops of capsicums and remove seeds
- Microwave on high for 4 minutes
- Place in a lightly greased oven dish and fill with meat mixture
- Bake at 180°C (360°F) for at least one hour
- Will keep in oven for 30 minutes longer if necessary

Serves 6
Approximate carbohydrate value per serve: ½ exchange
Per serve: P—32.2 g; F—8.7 g; CHO—7.0 g; KJ—990 (C—237)

Passover (Pesach)

Daphne's Salmon Rissoles (*pareve*)

Passover Chopped Herring (*pareve*)

Kneidlach (Matzah Balls) (*pareve*)

Eggplant (Aubergine) Patties (*pareve*)

Kichlach (*pareve*)

Pesach Rolls (*pareve*)

Apple Latkes (*pareve*)

Pesach Pastry (*pareve*)

Daphne's Salmon Rissoles *(pareve)*

Ingredients

420 g (14 oz) tin salmon (check availability of tinned
salmon in your area during Pesach)

1 egg

30 g (1 oz) onion, finely chopped or grated

Salt and pepper to taste

30 g (1 oz) matzah meal

Method

- Drain salmon but reserve liquid
- Remove skin and bones from fish
- Shred fish into small pieces
- Add reserved liquid and other ingredients and mix well
- Let stand for about 15 minutes until matzah meal has stiffened the mixture
- Shape into 6-8 rissoles and flatten them slightly
- Fry in a little oil till brown on both sides

Can be served hot or cold

Serves 4
Approximate carbohydrate value per rissole: 1/2 exchange
Per serve: P—23.3 g; F—12.7 g; CHO—7.5 g; KJ—990 (C—237)

Passover Chopped Herring *(pareve)*

● ●

Ingredients

500 g (1 lb 1 oz) matjes herring, rinsed and drained

4 hard-boiled eggs

150 g (5 oz) onions

300 g (10 oz) green apples

60 g (2 oz) matzah meal

75-120 ml (2-4 fl oz) vinegar according to taste

A little sugar to taste (sugar is used because

Splenda® is not suitable for Pesach)

Method

- Process all ingredients except vinegar and sugar together
- Add vinegar slowly ensuring that consistency is not sloppy
- Will keep in jars in fridge for several weeks

Serves 8
Approximate carbohydrate value per serve: 1 exchange
Per serve: P—17.3 g; F—18.6 g; CHO—18.5 g; KJ—1310 (C—313)

Kneidlach (Matzah Balls) *(pareve)*

Ingredients

375 g (13 oz) fine matzah meal

2 eggs

2 tablespoons margarine or pareve fat

500 ml (17 fl oz) boiling water

½ teaspoon salt

Method

- Melt fat or margarine in boiling water
- Add remaining ingredients and mix well
- Shape into 10-12 balls
- Keep in fridge for at least 6 hours
- Cook in boiling soup or salt water for 25 minutes
- Do not open the pot while kneidlach are cooking

Yields 12 kneidlach
Approximate carbohydrate value per kneidle: 1.5 exchanges
Per serve: P—4.5 g; F—3.9 g; CHO—24.3 g; KJ—610 (C—146)

Eggplant (Aubergine) Patties

(pareve)

● ●

Ingredients

375 g (13 oz) eggplant (aubergine),
   peeled and cubed

60 g (2 oz) matzah meal

50 g (1 ½ oz) onion, chopped finely

A little parsley

Garlic powder (optional)

Salt and pepper to taste

1 ½ tablespoons oil for frying

Method

- Boil eggplant (aubergine) till soft or microwave for 8 minutes
- Drain and mash or chop in processor
- Add matzah meal, onion, spices and seasoning
- Mix or process until well mixed
- Stand for 20-30 minutes to thicken
- Form into 6 patties
- Fry in oiled pan on medium heat till golden
- Serve with warm tomato sauce if desired

Yields 6 patties
Approximate carbohydrate value per patty: ½ exchange
Per serve: P—1.9 g; F—5.3 g; CHO—9.8 g; KJ—390 (C—93)

Kichlach *(pareve)*

● ●

Ingredients

2 eggs

1 tablespoon sugar (scant)

100 g (3 ⅓ oz) fine matzah meal

1 tablespoon oil

Method

- Mix all ingredients together well, adding more matzah meal if necessary
- Roll out dough on dry board with rolling pin till quite thin
- Cut into diamond shapes
- Brush with oil
- Bake at 250°C (490°F) on highest oven shelf for 2-3 minutes or until crisp
- Watch carefully as kichlach cook quickly
- Will keep for some weeks in an airtight container

To be eaten with chopped herring or chopped liver (pâté)

Yields about 20 kichlach
Approximate carbohydrate value per kichel: ½ exchange
Per serve: P—1.2 g; F—1.6 g; CHO—4.7; KJ—150 (C—43)

Pesach Rolls *(pareve)*

●●●●●●●●●●●●●●●●●●●●●●●●●●●●●●

Ingredients

120 ml (4 fl oz) water

60 ml (2 fl oz) oil

125 g (4 oz) matzah meal

½ teaspoon sugar

½ teaspoon salt

2 eggs

Method

- Boil oil and water and remove from heat
- Add matzah meal, salt and sugar
- Add eggs one at a time, beating well after each addition
- Leave to rest for half an hour
- Form into 6 round, unflattened balls
- Bake at 180°C (360°F) for 30 minutes
- Serve hot

Note: Recipe can be doubled

Yields 6 rolls
Approximate carbohydrate value per roll: 1 exchange
Per serve: P—4.4 g; F—11.9 g; CHO—16.8 g; KJ—780 (C—187)

Apple Latkes *(pareve)*

Ingredients

220 g (7 oz) green apples

30 g (1 oz) matzah meal

¼ teaspoon cinnamon

25 ml (1 fl oz) oil or pareve fat

A little sugar if necessary

Method

- Grate apples on a coarse grater
- Mix all ingredients together but only add the sugar if necessary
- Let stand for 20-30 minutes to allow mixture to stiffen
- Spoon into an oiled pan and cook over a medium heat for a few minutes
- Flip over and cook the other side
- Serve hot with strawberries or low-joule (low-calorie) jam

Yields 8 latkes
Approximate carbohydrate value per latke: ½ exchange
Per serve: P—0.5 g; F—3.2 g; CHO—6.3 g; KJ—230 (C—55)

Pesach Pastry *(pareve)*

Ingredients

125 g (4 oz) fine matzah meal

50 g (1 ½ oz) potato starch

½ teaspoon salt

2 teaspoons lemon juice

35 ml (1 fl oz) iced water

125 g (4 oz) margarine

Method

- Mix dry ingredients together
- Rub in margarine
- Add lemon juice and some of the water and mix well
- Add more water if mixture seems too dry
- Roll into a ball and cover with foil or cling wrap
- Refrigerate for at least half an hour
- Place in pie dish pushing into shape
- Put in any filling of choice
- Bake at 210°C (410°F) for 35-40 minutes

Pastry can be kept in fridge for a few days

Serves 8
Approximate carbohydrate value per serve: 1 exchange
Per serve: P—1.8 g; F—12.8 g; CHO—17.3 g; KJ—790 (C—189)

Pasta and Rice

Pasta and Salmon Salad (*pareve*)

Pasta Provencale (*pareve*)

Chicken and Pasta (*meat*)

Meatballs and Spaghetti (*meat*)

Macaroni Cheese (*milk*)

Baked Rice (*pareve or meat*)

Easy Rice Pilaf (*pareve or meat*)

Spanish Rice (*pareve*)

Pasta and Salmon Salad *(pareve)*

● ●

Ingredients

185 g (6 oz) dry pasta, cooked al dente and drained
(400 g/13 oz cooked)

415 g (14 oz) tin salmon, drained and roughly shredded

Method

- Mix cooked pasta and shredded salmon together

Dressing Ingredients

1 teaspoon dry mustard

1 teaspoon curry powder

2 teaspoons Splenda®

3 tablespoons white vinegar

1 tablespoon oil

1 tablespoon white wine

2 tablespoons tomato paste

Method

- Combine dressing ingredients and mix till smooth
- Pour over pasta mixture and mix well
- Chill

Variation

Add raw vegetables such as cucumber, mushrooms, tomatoes
and capsicum, thinly sliced before adding dressing.

Serves 9
Approximate carbohydrate value per serve: 1 exchange
Per serve: P—9.1 g; F—6.2 g; CHO—15.1 g; KJ—650 (C—155)

Pasta Provencale *(pareve)*

Ingredients

1 tablespoon olive oil

220 g (7 oz) eggplant (aubergine), chopped (leave skin on)

150 g (5 oz) red capsicum, chopped

150 g (5 oz) zucchini, sliced

100 g (3 ⅓ oz) onion, chopped

1 large clove garlic, chopped (optional)

400 g (13 oz) tin tomatoes, chopped

150 ml (5 fl oz) hot vegetable stock made from a cube

1 tablespoon tomato puree

½ teaspoon oregano leaves

½ teaspoon basil leaves

Freshly ground black pepper

Salt to taste

250 g (8 oz) pasta, your choice of kind

Method

- Heat a medium-sized pot and then add the oil
- Add the eggplant, capsicum, onion and garlic and cook until soft, about 5 minutes
- Add tomatoes, stock, puree and herbs
- Season to taste
- Cover and simmer for about 30 minutes
- Cook pasta in boiling water till al dente and drain
- Toss into the vegetable mixture
- Serve at once

Serves 4

Approximate carbohydrate value per serve: 3.5 exchanges
Per serve: P—10.2 g; F—6.4 g; CHO—52.5 g; KJ—1305 (C—312)

Chicken and Pasta *(meat)*

Ingredients

180 g (6 oz) noodles

1 clove garlic, chopped

1 small knob fresh ginger, chopped

125 g (4 oz) capsicum, chopped

90 g (3 oz) onion, chopped

60 g (2 oz) mushrooms, chopped

1 teaspoon curry powder

1 teaspoon paprika

500 g (1 lb 1 oz) chicken breast, cut into bite-sized
    pieces

50 g (1 ½ oz) tomato paste

3 tablespoons soy sauce

50 ml (1 ½ fl oz) white wine

100 ml (3 fl oz) water

Method

- Boil noodles till they are al dente and keep hot
- Fry vegetables in a little oil with curry powder and
  paprika till golden
- Add chicken pieces and fry till almost done
- Add tomato paste, soy sauce, wine and water
  mixed together
- When chicken is done, serve over noodles

Serves 4
Approximate carbohydrate value per serve: 2.5 exchanges
Per serve: P—36.1 g; F—3.7 g; CHO—36.2 g; KJ—1400 (C—335)

Meatballs and Spaghetti *(meat)*

Ingredients

500 g (1 lb 1 oz) lean mince
75 ml (2 ½ fl oz) iced water
½ teaspoon salt
¼ teaspoon pepper
70 g (2 ⅓ oz) onion, chopped finely
1 tablespoon oil

Method

- Mix all ingredients, except oil, together and shape into 24 meatballs
- Brown slowly in oil and remove from pan.

Sauce Ingredients

70 g (2 ⅓ oz) onion, chopped finely
2 cloves garlic, crushed
50 g (1 ½ oz) tomato paste
100 ml (3 fl oz) water or stock
50 ml (1 ½ fl oz) red wine
2 bay leaves
50 g (1 ½ oz) chopped parsley (optional)

Method

- Mix together and simmer in meatball drippings till thickened, stirring occasionally
- Add meatballs and simmer a little longer, about 10 minutes
- Serve hot over cooked spaghetti or preferred pasta

Serves 12
Approximate carbohydrate value per serve: negligible
Per serve: P—29.7 g; F—5.0 g; CHO—1.0 g; KJ—720 (C—172)

Macaroni Cheese *(milk)*

Ingredients

250 g (8 oz) pasta (macaroni, noodles or shells)

150 ml (5 fl oz) low-fat milk

2 level tablespoons cornflour (cornstarch)

125 g (4 oz) low-fat grated cheese

Salt and pepper to taste

Dash of cayenne pepper if desired

Method

- Boil pasta in salted water till almost done, drain well
- Make a thin paste of the milk and cornflour
- Heat slowly to avoid lumps forming
- Add grated cheese and stir well taking care not to burn mixture
- Add extra milk if sauce seems too thick
- Mix pasta and cheese sauce together
- Bake in suitable dish at 180°C (360°F) for about 40 minutes till top is crusty and brown
- Freezes well before baking
- Defrost completely before baking

Serves 7
Approximate carbohydrate value per serve: 2 exchanges
Per serve: P—10.4 g; F—8.4 g; CHO—29.4 g; KJ—990 (C—237)

Note: Cheese is high in saturated fat so it is desirable for diabetics to limit their intake.

Baked Rice

(pareve or meat, depending on cube used)

Ingredients

1 teaspoon oil

200 g (7 oz) rice

40 g (1 ⅓ oz) chopped onion

500 ml (17 fl oz) chicken or vegetable stock or water

Salt, pepper and cinnamon to taste

40 g (1 ⅓ oz) nuts, preferably cashew, optional

40 g (1 ⅓ oz) sultanas, optional

Method

- Preheat oven to 210°C (410°F)
- Stirring constantly, brown the rice and onion in oil till rice is coffee coloured
- Remove from heat and add seasoning, nuts and sultanas and the liquid
- Place in uncovered ovenproof dish and cook for 35 minutes

Serves 6
Approximate carbohydrate value per serve: 2 exchanges
Per serve: P—3.6 g; F—4.3 g; CHO—26.3 g; KJ—770 (C—184)

Easy Rice Pilaf

(pareve or meat, depending on cube used)

Ingredients

15 ml (½ fl oz) olive oil

30 g (1 oz) onion, chopped

1 small clove garlic (optional)

150 g (5 oz) rice

400 ml (13 fl oz) hot stock made from a cube

1 bay leaf

Pinch of pepper

Method

- Heat oil in suitable sized pot
- Add onion (and garlic) and cook on low till golden
- Add rice and sauté on low till almost milky white
- Add stock, bay leaf and pepper
- Allow to boil and then turn down to simmer
- Stir once with a fork and cover with lid
- Cook on low heat without stirring until liquid is absorbed, about 18 minutes
- Adjust seasoning if necessary

Note: Other vegetables such as diced carrots and celery can be added with the onions

Serves 6
Approximate carbohydrate value per serve: 1.5 exchanges
Per serve: P—1.8 g; F—2.7 g; CHO—20.1 g; KJ—470 (C—112)

Spanish Rice *(pareve)*

Ingredients

1 tablespoon olive oil

50 g (1 ½ oz) onion, chopped

1 clove garlic, chopped

50 g (1 ½ oz) capsicum, roughly chopped

50 g (1 ½ oz) mushroom, roughly chopped

75 g (2 ½ oz) celery, chopped

120 g (4 oz) tomato, roughly chopped

Salt and pepper to taste

A little dried oregano

250 g (8 oz) cooked rice

4 olives, roughly chopped

Method

- Brown onion and garlic in oil till just turning golden
- Add vegetables, salt and pepper and oregano
- Cook gently until done
- Add rice and mix in thoroughly until hot
- Add olives and adjust seasoning if necessary

Serves 6
Approximate carbohydrate value per serve: 1 exchange
Per serve: P—1.2 g; F—3.7 g; CHO—13.2 g; KJ—400 (C—96)

Poultry and Veal

Chicken Rachi

Chicken Burgers

Pan-grilled Chicken

Sherried Chicken

Spanish Chicken

Lemon Chicken

Chicken Curry

Veal and Vegetables

Veal Goulash

Chicken Rachi

Ingredients

1 kg (2 lbs 2 oz) boneless, skinned chicken

2 heaped teaspoons cornflour (cornstarch)

2 tablespoons soy sauce

1 tablespoon vegetable oil for frying

Method

- Cut chicken into bite-sized pieces
- Blend cornflour (cornstarch) with soy sauce and pour over chicken pieces in a large bowl
- Stir to coat the chicken
- Fry chicken in non-stick pan with thin layer of oil until golden brown all over
- Take care not to overcook
- Remove chicken with slotted spoon and keep warm in serving bowl

Sauce Ingredients

140 g (4 ⅔ oz) tomato paste

150 ml (5 fl oz) water

150 ml (5 fl oz) red wine

1 teaspoon Worcestershire sauce

2 heaped teaspoons Splenda® (optional)

Method

- Blend sauce ingredients, preferably in a blender or food processor
- Heat until just on the boil. This may be done in a microwave oven
- Pour over the cooked chicken and serve

Note: This recipe can be made with veal

Serves 8
Approximate carbohydrate value per serve: negligible
Per serve: P—29.1 g; F—5.4 g; CHO—3.0 g; KJ—800 (C—191)

Chicken Burgers

Ingredients

28 g (1 oz) breadcrumbs

500 g (1 lb 1 oz) chicken mince

1 teaspoon onion, finely chopped

1 tablespoon parsley, finely chopped

Salt and pepper to taste

1 tablespoon oil

Method

- Mix all ingredients, except oil, together well
- Form into 6 patties
- Fry in the oil on both sides till done

Yields 6 burgers
Approximate carbohydrate value per burger: negligible
Per serve: P—19.4 g; F—5.4 g; CHO—2.4 g; KJ—570 (C—136)

Pan-grilled Chicken (or Veal)

Ingredients

500 g (1 lb 1 oz) chicken breasts, or boneless veal
cutlets

90 g (3 oz) chopped onion

2 cloves garlic, chopped

¼ teaspoon each of thyme, coriander, marjoram
or mixed herbs

Dash of nutmeg

Salt and pepper to taste (optional)

50 ml (1 ½ fl oz) brown vinegar

100 ml (3 fl oz) red wine

100 ml (3 fl oz) water

1 tablespoon oil

Method

- Slice chicken breasts and sear in a large non-stick pan brushed lightly with olive oil
- Remove to a suitable serving dish
- Sauté spices, onions and garlic in any juices left in pan or add a teaspoon of oil
- Pour in liquids and allow to reduce by half
- Pour over chicken and serve

Serves 4
Approximate carbohydrate value per serve: negligible
Per serve: P—28.8 g; F—8.0 g; CHO—1.2 g; KJ—880 (C—210)

Sherried Chicken

Ingredients

1.2 kg (2 ½ lb) chicken fillets

Paprika, salt and pepper

30 ml (1 fl oz) oil

250 g (8 oz) sliced mushrooms

35 g (1 oz) chopped shallots

25 g (1 oz) flour

200 ml (7 fl oz) chicken stock

100 ml (3 fl oz) sherry

Method

- Sprinkle chicken with paprika, salt and pepper to taste
- Brown chicken in the oil till a nice colour
- Transfer to a suitable casserole dish
- Add mushrooms and shallots to the pan and cook until just tender
- Sprinkle with a little flour and stir in the stock and sherry
- Cook sauce for a few minutes stirring all the time
- Pour sauce over chicken and add more stock and/or sherry if it seems sparse
- Cover casserole and cook at 190°C (380°F) for 1 hour or until chicken is tender

Serves 10
Approximate carbohydrate value per serve: negligible
Per serve: P—30.2 g; F—13.4 g; CHO—2.4 g; KJ—1090 (C—261)

Spanish Chicken

Ingredients

1.2 kg (2 ½ lb) chicken fillets

Salt, pepper and paprika to taste

30 ml (1 fl oz) olive oil

50 g (1 ½ oz) finely chopped onion

2 cloves garlic, finely chopped

2 bay leaves

150 g (5 oz) green capsicum, finely chopped

2 x 440 g (15 oz) tins tomatoes

2 chicken stock cubes

100 ml (3 fl oz) water

¼ teaspoon saffron or turmeric (optional)

½ teaspoon dried oregano

Red capsicum or parsley, to garnish

Method

- Heat oven to 130°C (275°F)
- Sprinkle chicken lightly with salt, pepper and paprika
- Brown in heated olive oil on top of stove
- Place chicken into a suitable casserole
- Add onion, garlic, bay leaves and capsicum to pan on top of stove and cook for 3-5 minutes
- Add tomatoes and crumbled stock cubes
- Stir for about 5 minutes or until most of the meat drippings are loosened
- Stir in the water, saffron or turmeric, oregano and salt to taste

- Pour this sauce over the chicken, cover and bake for
  25 minutes
- Remove from oven and stir
- Return to oven and bake for another 30-35 minutes or until
  chicken is tender
- Garnish with strips of red capsicum or chopped parsley if
  desired

Can be kept in a very low oven for about 30 minutes if
necessary

Variation

200 g (7 oz) frozen peas can be added before last 20 minutes
of cooking.

Serves 10
Approximate carbohydrate value per serve: negligible
Per serve: P—30.0 g; F—13.5 g; CHO—3.4 g; KJ—1070 (C—256)

Lemon Chicken

● ●

Ingredients

75 g (2 ½ oz) flour

½ teaspoon salt

1 teaspoon paprika

750 g (1 lb 9 oz) chicken pieces or 500 g (1 lb 1 oz)
chicken breasts cut into suitable pieces

Juice from half a lemon

1 ½ tablespoons oil

1 chicken cube

175 ml (5 ½ fl oz) boiling water

3 chopped shallots

2 teaspoons grated lemon rind

Splenda® to adjust flavour if necessary

Method

- Mix flour, salt and paprika in a plastic bag
- Brush chicken with lemon juice
- Coat chicken with flour mixture in batches in the plastic bag and shake off excess
- Brown in a little oil in a heavy, non-stick pan
- Dissolve the chicken cube in the boiling water and pour over the chicken
- Stir in the shallots and the lemon rind
- Cook, covered, over a low heat for about 20 minutes or until chicken is done
- Add a little water if necessary and stir well
- Adjust flavour by adding a little salt and Splenda® if necessary

Note: Veal can be substituted if desired

Serves 6
Approximate carbohydrate value per serve: ½ exchange
Per serve: P—25.5 g; F—12.0 g; CHO—9.4 g; KJ—1040 (C—249)

Chicken Curry

Ingredients

800 g (1 lb 10 oz) chicken breasts, cut into bite sized
pieces

1 ½ tablespoons oil

30 g (1 oz) onion, finely chopped

1 clove garlic, finely chopped

2-4 teaspoon curry powder or to taste

100 g (3 ⅓ oz) mashed banana

140 g (4 ⅔ oz) green apple, grated or finely chopped

10 g (⅓ oz) low-joule (low-calorie) apricot jam

2 bay leaves

4 peppercorns

Juice of 1 small lemon

250 ml (8 fl oz) chicken stock

1 teaspoon Splenda®

Method

- Lightly brown chicken pieces in a little oil and set aside
- Fry onion and garlic together in the drippings
- Add curry powder and stir well
- Add rest of ingredients, slowly mixing well
- Bring to boil and simmer for about 5 minutes
- Add chicken and simmer till chicken is heated through
- Adjust seasoning if necessary
- Thicken sauce with a little cornflour (cornstarch) if necessary

Note: Cooked diced chicken can be used and added to sauce
instead of raw chicken

Serves 6
Approximate carbohydrate value per serve: ½ exchange
Per serve: P—30.8 g; F—8.4 g; CHO—7.5 g; KJ—960 (C—230)

Veal with Vegetables

Ingredients

½ teaspoon salt

¼ teaspoon pepper

¼ teaspoon paprika

500 g (1 lb 1 oz) boneless veal cut into 5 equal
portions

30 g (1 oz) low-fat pareve margarine or 30 ml
(1 fl oz) olive oil

4 tinned tomatoes

12 spears asparagus (optional)

125 g (4 oz) sliced mushrooms

Method

- Sprinkle salt, pepper and paprika over veal
- Sauté veal in margarine or oil till browned
- Place one tomato, 3 asparagus spears and a heaped
  tablespoon mushrooms on each piece
- Cook over medium heat, very gently spooning juices over
  meat continually
- Cook uncovered until meat is very tender

Serves 5
Approximate carbohydrate value per serve: negligible
Per serve: P—32.1 g; F—8.5 g; CHO—1.5 g; KJ—890 (C—213)

Veal Goulash

Ingredients

200 g (7 oz) onion, chopped fine

1 clove garlic, chopped

2 teaspoons oil

1 kg (2 lbs 2 oz) veal, cubed

50 g (1 ½ oz) tomato paste

1 ½ teaspoons paprika

1 teaspoon caraway seed (optional)

2 bay leaves

300 ml (10 fl oz) water or stock

Salt and pepper to taste

10 g (⅓ oz) cornflour (cornstarch)

25 ml (1 fl oz) water or vinegar

Chopped parsley for garnish

Method

- Fry the onions and garlic in a little oil till transparent but not brown
- Add meat and brown a little
- Add tomato paste, paprika, caraway, bay leaf and the water or stock
- Cook gently till meat is tender, stirring occasionally
- Add salt and pepper to taste
- Dissolve cornflour (cornstarch) in the water or vinegar and add slowly to meat
- Stir carefully until sauce has thickened

Serves 8
Approximate carbohydrate value per serve: negligible
Per serve: P—29.6 g; F—3.6 g; CHO—2.9 g; KJ—680 (C—163)

Salads and Dressings

Green Bean Salad (*pareve*)

Curried Pineapple (*pareve*)

Salad Dressing (*pareve*)

Coleslaw (*milk or pareve*)

Caesar Salad Dressing (*milk*)

Potato Salad (*milk*)

Green Bean Salad *(pareve)*

Ingredients

1 kg (2 lbs 2 oz) green beans

30 g (1 oz) onion, sliced thinly, preferably Spanish

Method

- Top and tail beans and cut into bite-sized pieces
- Boil in lightly salted water till done but still crisp, or microwave for 4-5 minutes with 15 ml (½ fl oz) water
- Add to onions

Marinade Ingredients

¼ cup (2 fl oz) olive oil

½ cup (4 fl oz) brown vinegar

1 large clove of garlic, finely crushed

½ teaspoon grain mustard

½ teaspoon dried tarragon

Lots of fresh ground black pepper

Method

- Whisk ingredients together very well
- Add to beans and onions
- Chill

Will keep for several days

Variation

Add 1 chopped fresh tomato (100 g/3 ½ oz) and 3 tablespoons (50 g/2 oz) chopped parsley

Serves 6

Approximate carbohydrate value per serve: ½ exchange

Per serve: P—3.8 g; F—10.3 g; CHO—4.3 g; KJ—540 (C—129)

Curried Pineapple *(pareve)*

Ingredients

1 small tin (440 g/15 oz) pineapple pieces in natural juice

6 tablespoons Splenda®

2 teaspoons curry powder

12 g (½ oz) cornflour

250 ml (8 fl oz) white wine

Method

- Drain pineapple, reserving liquid
- Mix Splenda®, curry powder and cornflour with a little pineapple liquid
- Add to the wine and boil for 2-3 minutes till thickened
- Pour over the pineapple
- Chill
- Will keep well for approximately a week

Serves 6
Approximate carbohydrate value per serve: 1 exchange.
(Smaller amounts, e.g. 1 tablespoon would be negligible.)
Per serve: P—0.6 g; F—0.1 g; CHO—11.4 g; KJ—320 (C—77)

Salad Dressing *(pareve)*

Ingredients

¼ cup (2 fl oz) olive oil

¾ cup (6 fl oz) of fresh lemon juice or vinegar

1 teaspoon salt

1 teaspoon black pepper

1 level teaspoon Splenda®

1 teaspoon comino (cumin) seeds

1 teaspoon marjoram

1 clove garlic, crushed

2 generous teaspoons oregano leaves

Method

- Shake all ingredients together well
- Chill
- Will keep for about a week in refrigerator

Serves 10
Approximate carbohydrate value per serve: negligible
Per serve: P—0 g; F —6.0 g; CHO—0.1 g; KJ—230 (C—55)

Coleslaw

(milk or pareve, depending on mayonnaise used)

Ingredients

600 g (1 lb 4 oz) white cabbage, finely shredded

2-3 teaspoons Splenda®

Method

- Sprinkle cabbage with Splenda® and leave to stand for several hours

Dressing Ingredients

½ cup (4 fl oz) light mayonnaise

5 tablespoons juice from pickled cucumbers with
  some
  of the seed

¼ teaspoon each of black pepper and grated onion

A little lemon juice, pinch of salt

Method

- Blend marinade ingredients well
- Pour over cabbage, cover and chill well

Serves 6
Approximate carbohydrate value per serve: ½ exchange
Per serve: P—1.6 g; F—4.3 g; CHO—7.5 g; KJ—320 (C—77)

Caesar Salad Dressing *(milk)*

Ingredients

1 medium clove of garlic

1-2 strips anchovy fillets (according to taste)

15 ml (½ fl oz) milk, plain low-fat yoghurt or
buttermilk

½ tablespoon lemon juice

¼ teaspoon mild mustard

3 tablespoons olive oil

Method

- Blend all ingredients in a processor until very smooth
- Pour over lettuce pieces and serve chilled

Serve 4
Approximate carbohydrate value per serve: negligible
Per serve: P—0.8 g; F—15.2 g; CHO—0.4 g; KJ—580 (C—139)

Potato Salad *(milk)*

Ingredients

480 g (1 lb) cooked potatoes, peeled and diced

30 g (1oz) shallots or onion, chopped roughly

Dressing Ingredients

125 ml (4 fl oz) light mayonnaise

Pinch basil leaves

Ground pepper to taste

15 ml (½ fl oz) juice from pickled cucumbers or
lemon juice

15 ml (½ fl oz) low-fat milk

1 teaspoon Splenda® if desired

Method

- Shake well together and add to potatoes
- Sprinkle with paprika
- Chill

Variations

- Add 45 g (1 ½ oz) cooked peas can be added if desired
- Add 1 grated green apple for a sweet and sour flavour

Serves 4
Approximately carbohydrate value per serve: 1.5 exchanges
(2 with apple)
Per serve (no apple): P—3.4 g; F—6.9 g; CHO—23.6 g; KJ—720
(C—172)
Per serve (with apple): P—3.7 g; F—6.9 g; CHO—27.8 g; KJ—790
(C—189)

Sauces and Marinades

Monkey Gland Sauce (*pareve*)

Mexican Sauce (*pareve*)

Daphne's Spaghetti Sauce (*pareve*)

Tomato Marinade (*pareve*)

Soy Marinade (*pareve*)

Monkey Gland Sauce

Ingredients

50 g (1 ½ oz) low-joule (low-calorie) apricot jam

25 g (1 oz) tomato sauce

3 tablespoons Worcestershire sauce

1 tablespoon white or brown vinegar

60 g (2 oz) onions, sliced

Salt, pepper, paprika to taste

Method

- Mix all ingredients together and use to marinate meat for at least one hour
- Remove meat and grill
- Simmer sauce till thickened
- Serve separately over meat

Note: Suitable for 400 g (13 oz) steak or meatballs

Serves 4
Approximate carbohydrate value per serve: ½ exchange
Per serve: P—0.6 g; F—0.1 g; CHO—7.7 g; KJ—140 (C—33)

Mexican Sauce *(pareve)*

Ingredients

100 ml (3 fl oz) oil

150 ml (5 fl oz) white vinegar

½ teaspoon salt

2 large cloves garlic, crushed

30 g (1 oz) parsley, finely chopped

½ teaspoon paprika

½ teaspoon ground cumin

¼ teaspoon chilli powder or cayenne pepper

½ teaspoon black pepper

15 g (½ oz) ground oregano

1 bay leaf, finely chopped

Method

- Mix all ingredients together well
- Bottle and shake thoroughly at once and whenever you remember afterwards
- Keep for at least 24 hours before using
- Will keep in fridge almost indefinitely
- Use as a marinade or to spice up Mexican food

Serves 16
Approximate carbohydrate value per serve: negligible
Per serve: P—0.1g; F—6.3 g; CHO—0 g; KJ—240 (C—57)

Daphne's Spaghetti Sauce *(pareve)*

Ingredients

400 g (13 oz) tin of tomatoes

150 g (5 oz) onion

10 g (⅓ oz) parsley (or more as desired)

1 clove garlic

Salt and pepper to taste

Oregano or other spice if desired

Method

- Process all ingredients together till finely chopped
- Boil down to half in volume
- Serve hot

Serves 3

Approximate carbohydrate value per serve: ½ exchange

Per serve: P—2.0 g; F—0.4 g; CHO—6.6 g; KJ—160 (C—38)

Tomato Marinade *(pareve)*

Ingredients

225 ml (7 ½ fl oz) tomato juice (unsweetened)

100 g (3 ⅓ oz) chopped onion

1 teaspoon dried basil

1 teaspoon Splenda®

1 teaspoon chopped garlic or garlic powder

Method

- Mix all ingredients together in a bowl
- Add meat and allow to marinate for at least one hour
- Grill or fry meat in a non-stick pan
- Heat remaining marinade and use as a sauce if desired

Note: Suitable for 500 g (1 lb 1 oz) meat

Serves 3
Approximate carbohydrate value per serve: ½ exchange
Per serve: P—1.1 g; F—0.1 g; CHO—4.5 g; KJ—100 (C—24)

Soy Marinade *(pareve)*

● ●

Ingredients

1 tablespoon olive oil

1 teaspoon lemon juice

30 ml (1 fl oz) soy sauce

1 level tablespoon Splenda®

1 tablespoon chopped or grated onion

¼ teaspoon garlic salt or garlic flakes

¼ teaspoon ground ginger

¼ teaspoon black pepper

Method

- Mix all ingredients together well
- Pour over two pieces of meat and leave for at least one hour before grilling

Serves 2
Approximate carbohydrate value per serve: negligible
Per serve: P—0.9 g; F—10.0 g; CHO—1.6 g; KJ—420 (C—100)

Soups

Mexican Meatball Soup

Quick Minestrone (*pareve*)

Sweet Corn Soup (*milk*)

Gazpacho (*pareve*)

Mexican Meatball Soup

Ingredients

750 g (1 lb 9 oz) best lean mince

30 g (1 oz) flour

2 eggs

1 ½ litres (50 fl oz) chicken broth (made from cubes)

1 litre (33 fl oz) beef broth (made from cubes)

175 g (5 ½ oz) onions, chopped

1 teaspoon chilli powder

1 teaspoon dried oregano leaves

350 g (12 oz) carrots, sliced thinly

50 g (1 ½ oz) long grain rice

2 teaspoons coriander, fresh if possible

175 g (5 ½ oz) washed and roughly shredded spinach

2-3 limes or 2 lemons cut into wedges (optional)

Method

- Combine well meat, flour, eggs and 125 ml (4 fl oz) of the chicken broth in a bowl
- In a large pot combine remaining broth, oregano, onions, and chilli
- Bring to the boil then simmer on low heat
- Shape beef into smallish balls dropping each into the broth
- Simmer uncovered for 5 minutes skimming off any fat or foam
- Add carrots, rice and coriander and simmer for about 20 minutes till carrots are tender
- Add spinach to soup and cook for another 5 minutes
- Serve with lemon or lime wedges if desired

Yields 20 meatballs
Approximate carbohydrate value per serve: almost ½ exchange
Per serve: P—9.5 g; F—2.0 g; CHO—4.4 g; KJ—310 (C—74)

Quick Minestrone *(pareve)*

Ingredients

3 vegetable stock cubes

1 ½ litres (2 ½ pt) boiling water

40 g (1 ⅓ oz) chopped onion

25 g (1 oz) chopped parsley

80 g (2 ½ oz) chopped celery leaves

300 g (10 oz) chopped ripe tomatoes

50 g (1 ½ oz) shredded cabbage

1 x 300 g (10 oz) tin red kidney beans, drained

120 g (4 oz) noodles of any sort

2 bay leaves

Salt and pepper to taste

Method

- Dissolve cubes in boiling water
- Add all ingredients and cook till noodles are done
- Serve with grated low-fat cheese if desired

Serves 6
Approximate carbohydrate value per serve: 1.5 exchanges
Per serve: P—5.2 g; F—0.5 g; CHO—20 g; KJ—450 (C—108)

Sweet Corn Soup *(milk)*

● ●

Ingredients

440 g (15 oz) tin corn kernels (creamed corn not
suitable)

500 ml (17 fl oz) low-fat milk

¼ teaspoon paprika

Dash of chilli powder or cayenne pepper to taste

Method

- Mix all ingredients together in blender or processor
- Heat gently but do not bring to the boil
- Adjust taste as desired

Serves 4
Approximate carbohydrate value per serve: 1.5 exchanges
Per serve: P—7.0 g; F—2.4 g; CHO—21.3 g; KJ—550 (C—132)

Gazpacho *(pareve)*

Ingredients

400 g (13 oz) tin tomatoes

400 g (13 oz) tin tomato puree

160 g (5 ⅓ oz) green capsicum

1 clove garlic

130 g (4 ⅓ oz) Lebanese cucumber

3 shallots

1 tablespoon olive oil

Splash of vinegar

Salt and pepper to taste

Spices to taste: oregano, thyme, mixed herbs

Method

- Liquidise all ingredients
- Chill

Freezes well

Serve 6
Approximate carbohydrate value per serve: ½ exchange
Per serve: P—2.1 g; F—3.6 g; CHO—6.8 g; KJ—290 (C—69)

Vegetables and Vegetarian

Indian Potato and Carrots (*pareve*)

Potato Latkes (*pareve*)

Glazed Carrots (*pareve*)

Hush Puppies (*pareve*)

Green Beans in Tomato Sauce (*pareve*)

Red or White Cabbage (*pareve*)

Vegetable Casserole (*milk*)

Easy Potato Kugel (*pareve*)

Ratatouille (*pareve*)

Eggplant (Aubergine) Casserole (*pareve*)

Indian Potatoes and Carrots
(pareve)

● ●

Ingredients

360 g (12 oz) potatoes

500 g (1 lb 1 oz) carrots

20 ml (⅔ fl oz) oil

3 teaspoons cumin seeds

Chilli powder to taste

1 teaspoon ground coriander

¼ teaspoon turmeric

Salt to taste

50 ml (1 ½ fl oz) water

Juice of half a lemon

Method

- Peel and cube potatoes and carrots
- Heat oil in deep pan and add spices
- Stir-fry for 1-2 minutes
- Add potatoes and carrots and cover
- Cook on low heat for about 10 minutes or until vegetables are done
- Sprinkle with a little water if necessary
- Sprinkle with lemon juice just before serving

Serves 5
Approximate carbohydrate value per serve: 1 exchange
Per serve: P—2.5 g; F—4.1 g; CHO—14.5 g; KJ—450 (C—108)

Potato Latkes *(pareve)*

Ingredients

480 g (1 lb) potatoes, peeled and grated

50 g (1 ½ oz) onions, chopped or grated

40 g (1 ⅓ oz) flour

2 eggs

Salt and pepper to taste

1 ½ tablespoons oil

Method

- Mix all ingredients together well
- Fry tablespoonfuls in hot oil till nicely brown
- Serve hot

Yields 10
Approximate carbohydrate value per latke: ½ exchange
Per serve: P—2.71 g; F—4.02 g; CHO—8.78 g; KJ—350 (C—84)

Glazed Carrots *(pareve)*

Ingredients

300 g (10 oz) carrots, sliced

15 g (½ oz) margarine

Dash of ginger

3 tablespoons Splenda®

45 ml (1 ½ fl oz) orange juice

15 ml (½ fl oz) water

Method

- Cook carrots and water in microwave till almost done
- Drain excess water
- Add other ingredients and cook for a few more minutes

Serves 2
Approximate carbohydrate value per serve: 1 exchange
Per serve: P—1.4 g; F—6.2 g; CHO—12.3 g; KJ—460 (C—110)

Hush Puppies *(pareve)*

● ●

Ingredients

440 ml (14 ½ fl oz) tin corn kernels, drained

1 egg

30 g (1 oz) chopped onion or shallots

125 g (4 oz) flour

Seasoning to taste

1 tablespoon oil for frying

Method

- Mix all ingredients, except oil, together
- Heat non-stick pan and add oil when pan is warm
- Fry tablespoonfuls of mixture, flattening them slightly
- Serve hot

Yields 10 fritters
Approximate carbohydrate value per fritter: 1 exchange
Per serve: P—2.9 g; F—2.9 g; CHO—14.6 g; KJ—400 (C—96)

Green Beans in Tomato Sauce
(pareve)

Ingredients

350 g (12 oz) green beans

15 ml (½ fl oz) olive oil

80 g (2 ½ oz) onion, chopped roughly

1 large clove garlic, chopped roughly

400 g (13 oz) tomato, tinned or fresh, chopped
roughly (drain if tinned)

125 ml (4 fl oz) water

1 tablespoon tomato paste

2 tablespoons chopped parsley

Fresh ground black pepper

Salt and oregano to taste (optional)

Method

- Top and tail beans and cut into 3-5 cm (1 ½-2 in) pieces
- Heat pan and then add oil
- Lightly fry onion and garlic till almost golden brown
- Add other ingredients and cover pan
- Cook gently for about 15 minutes, more if you want the beans soft
- Can be served hot, warm or cold

Serves 4
Approximate carbohydrate value per serve: ½ exchange
Per serve: P—3.5 g; F—4.2 g; CHO—6.8 g; KJ—330 (C—79)

Red or White Cabbage *(pareve)*

Ingredients

75 g (2 ½ oz) onion, chopped

3 teaspoons olive oil for cooking

500 g (1 lb 1 oz) cabbage, shredded finely

300 g (10 oz) green apples, peeled, cored and cut
into eighths

125 ml (4 fl oz) vinegar

125 ml (4 fl oz) water

2 teaspoons salt

10 g (⅓ oz) Splenda® depending on taste

Method

- Fry onions in oil till just transparent
- Add cabbage, apples, vinegar and water
- Cook on low for about 20-30 minutes stirring frequently
  till cabbage is tender
- Add Splenda® and salt and adjust taste by adding more
  vinegar or Splenda®
- Can be served hot or cold

Serves 6
Approximate carbohydrate value per serve: ½ exchange
Per serve: P—1.6 g; F—2.7 g; CHO—9.2 g; KJ—290 (C—69)

Vegetable Casserole *(milk)*

Ingredients

120 g (4 oz) carrots

240 g (8 oz) potatoes

125 g (4 oz) corn, fresh or tinned (drained)

75 g (2 ½ oz) capsicum

160 g (5 ⅓ oz) any other vegetable you choose

25 ml (1 fl oz) olive or salad oil

50 g (1 ½ oz) onion, chopped

1 clove garlic, chopped

100 ml (3 fl oz) vegetable stock or water

30 g (1 oz) low-fat grated cheese

Method

- Slice all vegetables
- Heat oil in casserole
- Toss onion and garlic in oil until golden
- Add other vegetables and stir till all covered with oil
- Season as desired, e.g. spices, curry powder, salt and pepper
- Pour stock or water over and cover casserole dish
- Cook at 180°C (360°F) for about 75 minutes
- Remove lid and sprinkle with cheese
- Brown for a few minutes

Serves 4
Approximate carbohydrate value per serve: 1 exchange
Per serve: P—6.9 g; F—8.5 g; CHO—15.9 g; KJ—710 (C—170)

Easy Potato Kugel *(pareve)*

● ●

Ingredients

240 g (8 oz) potato

25 g (1 oz) onion

130 g (4 ⅓ oz) carrot

½ teaspoon salt

Pepper to taste

1 tablespoon vegetable stock or water

1 tablespoon oil

25 g (1 oz) matzah meal (can be added if desired)

Method

- Preheat oven to 190°C (380°F)
- Peel and grate vegetables
- Mix all ingredients together
- Place in a well-oiled casserole
- Dot with a little margarine or drizzle a little oil over the top
- Bake for 1 hour
- Serve hot

Heats up well in microwave

Serves 2
Approximate carbohydrate value per serve: 1.5 exchanges
Per serve: P—3.5 g; F—10.1 g; CHO—19.6 g; KJ—780 (C—187)

Ratatouille *(pareve)*

Ingredients

1 tablespoon olive oil

100 g (3 ⅓ oz) onion, chopped

1 large clove garlic, chopped

850 g (1 lb 12 oz) mixed vegetables, chopped: celery,
carrots, capsicum, zucchini, cauliflower, broccoli

2 slices ginger, chopped (optional)

1 tablespoon dried basil

2 bay leaves

4 peppercorns

450 g (15 oz) eggplant (aubergine), cubed with
skin left on

400 g (13 oz) tin tomatoes

400 g (13 oz) tin tomato puree

50 g (1 ½ oz) tomato paste

50 ml (1 ½ fl oz) red wine (optional)

50 ml (1 ½ fl oz) boiling water

200 ml (7 fl oz) water or vegetable stock

Method

- Brown onion, garlic, carrots and ginger in oil till onions are transparent
- Add basil, bay leaves and peppercorns and stir a little
- Add all vegetables and stir well
- Chop tomatoes with kitchen scissors
- Mix tomato paste with wine and boiling water and add to tomatoes
- Add this mixture to the vegetables and stir well
- Add puree to vegetables and stir well
- Cover and simmer till vegetables are tender, about 20-25 minutes

This freezes very well

Serves 12 large portions
Approximate carbohydrate value per serve: ½ exchange
Per serve: P—2.7 g; F—2.0 g; CHO—6.3 g; KJ—240 (C—57)

Eggplant (Aubergine) Casserole

(pareve)

● ●

Ingredients

100 g (3 ⅓ oz) mushrooms, chopped

30 g (1 oz) onion, chopped

1 clove garlic, chopped

400 g (13 oz) tin kidney beans, drained

400 g (13 oz) tin tomatoes, chopped

400 g (13 oz) eggplant (aubergine), sliced with
skin left on

Method

- Mix all ingredients, except eggplant (aubergine), together.
  Mixture shouldn't be too sloppy
- Put layers of eggplant (aubergine) and mixture in oiled
  casserole ending with eggplant (aubergine)

Topping Ingredients

200 g (7 oz) plain low-fat yoghurt

1 egg

60 g (2 oz) low-fat grated cheese

Method

- Mix all ingredients together well
- Spoon over casserole
- Bake at 160°C (310°F) for 1 ½ hours or at 180°C (360°F)
  for 40 minutes

Serves 6

Approximate carbohydrate value per serve: ½ exchange
Per serve: P—4.8 g; F—0.7 g; CHO—10.1 g; KJ—280 (C—67)

Handy Hints

- Parsley will keep fresh if stored in the fridge in an airtight jar. The stalks have all the flavour so use these for soups and stews and the heads for garnish.
- To make egg whites easy to beat, have them at room temperature and add a pinch of salt.
- When frying fish, add a little curry powder to the pan; it prevents the fishy odour and improves the colour and flavour of the fish.
- To extract more juice from a lemon, stand it in hot water for a few minutes first, or microwave it for a few seconds.
- To coat fish or meat evenly with flour, shake it in a plastic bag containing the flour with the seasoning added. Seeds (such as sesame seeds), grated low-fat cheese or crushed breakfast cereal added to the flour will give a different taste and appearance to fish.
- Use a dissolved soup cube for stir-frying instead of oil.
- Soak parsley in hot water before adding to a salad or salad dressing to enhance flavour.
- Add a few drops of lemon juice to cauliflower when cooking to keep it white.
- To prevent eggs from cracking during boiling, add a teaspoon of vinegar to the water.
- To cook 600 g (21 oz) frozen fish, microwave on high for 10-12 minutes.

Glossary

al dente This is Italian and means 'to the tooth'. It is used to describe spaghetti, lightly cooked so that it is a little chewy.

Ashkenazi (plural Ashkenazim) Jews tracing their descent from central and eastern Europe.

Diaspora The dispersion of Jews from their homeland; now refers to Jews not living in Israel.

exchange 1 exchange is equal to 15 g of carbohydrate.

farfel Grated pieces or crumbs of solid food such as matzo or biscuit (cookie) dough.

frikkadels South African term for hamburger patty.

gefilte fish Literally 'filled fish'. The flesh is minced and mixed with egg, meal and seasoning and either stuffed back into the fish skin and baked or made into balls and simmered in stock or salt water. Served cold.

Glycaemic Index (GI) A measure of the effect specific foods have on blood sugar level

hummus A dip made of ground chickpeas and seasoning.

kashrut The dietary laws prescribed by Jewish tradition.

kichel (plural kichlach) A small flat crisp biscuit (cookie) eaten with chopped herring, chopped liver (pâté) or hummus.

kneidle (plural kneidlach) Matzah balls.

kosher Applied to food allowed to be used according to Jewish dietary laws.

kugel A baked casserole of pasta or potato often referred to as 'pudding'.

latke A pancake, usually made of grated potato, egg and seasoning.

matjes herrings Herring fillets obtained in tins or vacuum packed in smaller packets, pickled in oil and spices or vinegar and spices.

matzah (matzo) Unleavened bread eaten at Passover.

matzah meal Ground up matzot (plural).

pareve (parave) Food that is neither milk nor meat, i.e. neutral, so it can be eaten with either.

Pesach (Passover) An important Jewish festival commemorating the exodus of the Children of Israel from Egyptian bondage.

Sephardi (plural Sephardim) Jews tracing their descent from Spain, Portugal and the Middle East.

shashlik (kebabs) Food cooked on a skewer.

Splenda® A low-kilojoule (low-calorie) sugar substitute made from sugar.

tamm (ta'am) A Yiddish word meaning taste or flavour.

Yiddish An old everyday language of Ashkenazic Jews, now enjoying a revival worldwide.

Metric/Imperial Conversion Tables (simplified)

Weight

Grams (g)	Kilograms (kg)	Imperial
30		1 oz
60		2 oz
120		4 oz
150		5 oz
200	0.2	7 oz
450	0.45	1 lb
500	0.5	1 lb 2 oz
1000	1	2 lb 4 oz
1400	1.4	3 lb
1800	1.8	4 lb

Volume

Millilitre (ml)	Litre (l)	Imperial (US)	Australian
5		1 teaspoon	1 teaspoon
15		1 tablespoon	1 tablespoon
30		1 fl oz	30 ml
60		2 fl oz	60 ml
100		3 fl oz	100 ml
125		4 fl oz	125 ml
250	0.25	8 fl oz, 1 cup	¾ cup
500	0.5	2 cups	1 ½ cups
600	0.6	1 pint	600 ml
1000	1	1 ¾ pints	1000 ml
1500	1.5	2 ½ pints	1500 ml

Temperature

Gas mark	Fahrenheit	Celsius (Centigrade)	
	150	65	
	200	90	
	210	100	
¼–½	250	125	Very slow (very cool)
1-2	300	145	Slow (cool)
3-4	325	165	Moderately slow (warm)
5	360	180	Moderate
6	400	205	Moderate
	430	220	Moderately hot
7-8	450	230	Hot
9-10	500	260	Very hot
	550	290	

Contact List

Kashrut

NSW Kashrut Authority
36 Flood Street
Bondi NSW 2026
AUSTRALIA
Tel: 61 (2) 9369 4286
Fax: 61 (2) 9369 4286
Email: rabbig@ka.or.au

Kashrut Division of the
London Beth Din
Court of the Chief Rabbi
Adler House
735 High Road
London N12 OUS
UK
Tel: 44 (20) 8343 6255
Fax: 44 (20) 8343 6254/56
Email: info@kosher.org.uk
Website: www.kosher.org.uk

Arlene J Mathes-Scharf
Food Scientist-Kosher Food
Specialist
Scharf Associates
PO Box 50
Sharon MA 02067
USA
Tel: 1 (781) 784 6890
Fax: 1 (781) 784 6890
Email: ajms@kashrut.com
Website: www.kashrut.com

Kosher Supervision of
America (KSA)
PO Box 35721
Los Angeles CA 35721

USA
Tel: 1 (310) 282 -444
Fax: 1 (310) 282 0505
Email: kosher@primenet.org
Website:
www.primenet.com/~kosher

The Union of Orthodox
Jewish Congregations
Eleven Broadway
New York NY 10004
USA
Kashrut Questions Hotline:
1 (212) 613 8241
Tel: 1 (212) 563 4000
Fax: 1 (212) 564 9054
Email: kosherq@ou.org
Website: www.ou.org

Diabetes

Diabetes Australia Call to
find the location of your
nearest diabetes educators
and dietitians.

DA National Office
Churchill House, 1st Floor
218 Northbourne Avenue
Braddon ACT 2612
AUSTRALIA
Tel: 61 (2) 6230 1155
Fax: 61 (2) 6230 1551
Email:
mail@diabetesaustralian.com.au
Website:
www.diabetesaustralia.com.au

DA Queensland
Cnr Ernest and Merivale
Streets
South Brisbane QLD 4101
AUSTRALIA
Tel: 61 (7) 3846 4600
Fax: 61 (7) 3846 4642
Email: daqld@daq.or.au

DA New South Wales
26 Arundel Street
Glebe NSW 2037
(GPO Box 9824 Sydney
NSW 2001)
AUSTRALIA
Tel: 1300 136 588 (Australia
only)
Tel: 61 (2) 9552 9900
Fax: 61 (2) 9660 3633
Email: dansw@talent.com.au

DA Victoria
3rd Floor, 100 Collins Street
Melbourne VIC 3000
(GPO Box 206D Melbourne
VIC 3001)
AUSTRALIA
Tel: 61 (3) 9654 8777
Fax: 61 (3) 9650 1917
Email: mail@dav.org.au
Website: www.dav.org.au

DA Northern Territory
2 Tiwi Place
Tiwi NT 0810
(PO Box 40113, Casuarina
NT 0811)
AUSTRALIA

Tel: 61 (8) 8927 8488/8482
Fax: 61 (8) 8927 8515
Email: ceo@diabetesnt.org.au

DA South Australia
159 Burbridge Road
Hilton SA 5033
(GPO Box 1930, Adelaide
SA 5001)
AUSTRALIA
Tel: 61 (8) 8234 1977
Fax: 61 (8) 8234 2013
Email: dasa@da-sa.com.au

DA Tasmania
57E Brisbane Street
Hobart TAS 7000
AUSTRALIA
Tel: 61 (3) 6234 5223
Fax: 61 (3) 6224 0105
Email: DATAS@bigpond.com.au

DA Western Australia
48 Wickham Street
(PO Box 6097)
East Perth WA 6004
AUSTRALIA
Tel: 61 (8) 9325 7699
Fax: 61 (8) 9221 1183

Canadian Diabetes
Association
15 Toronto Street
Suite 800
Toronto Ontario M5C E3
CANADA
Tel: 1 (416) 363 3373
Fax: 1 (416) 214 1899
Email: info@cda.nat.org
Website: www.diabetic.ca

Diabetic Association of Israel
46 Ha'maccabi
Rishon LeTzion 75359
ISRAEL
Tel: 972 (3) 950 8222
Fax: 972 (3) 950 8111

Diabetes Association of
South Africa
National Office
PO Box 1715
Saxonwold
Johannesburg 2132
SOUTH AFRICA
Tel: 27 (11) 788 4595
Fax: 27 (11) 447 5100

Diabetes UK
10 Queens Anne Street
London W1M OBD
UK

Tel: 44 (20) 7323 1531
Fax: 44 (20) 7462 2732
Email:
customerservice@diabetes.org.uk
Website: www.diabetes.org.uk

American Diabetes
Association
National Office
1701 North Beauregard
Street
Alexandria VA 22311
USA
Tel: 1 (800) 342 2383 (USA
only)
Email:
customerservice@diabetes.or
Website: www.diabetes.org

National Institute of
Diabetes & Digestive &
Kidney Diseases (NIDDK)
Office of Communications
and Public Liaison
NIDDK, NIH
31 Center Drive MSC 2560
Bethesda MD 20892-2560
USA
Website: www/niddk.nih.gov

Index